ETHICAL
DEBATES

Advertising

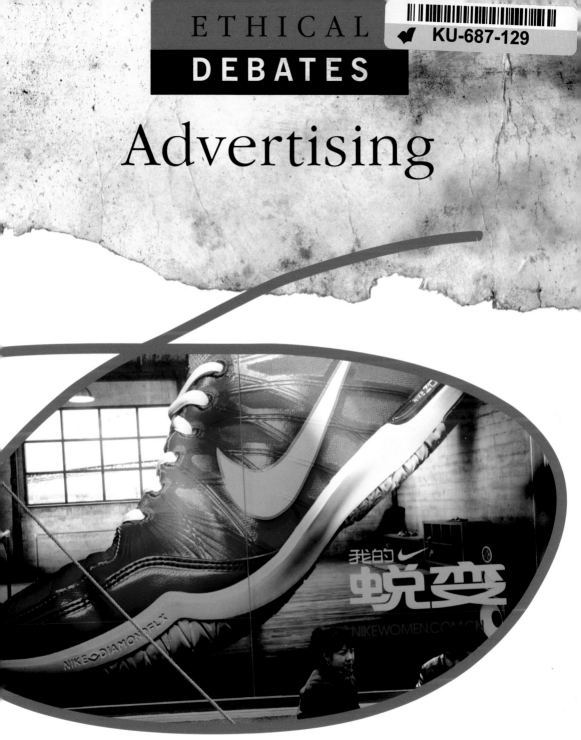

JEN GREEN

WAYLAND

First published in 2011 by Wayland
Copyright © 2011 Wayland

Wayland
338 Euston Road
London NW1 3BH

Wayland Australia
Level 17/207 Kent Street
Sydney NSW 2000

All rights reserved.

Editor: Julia Adams
Designer: Rita Storey
Picture researcher: Diana Morris
Indexer: Rebecca Clunes

British Library Cataloguing in Publication
data
Green, Jen.
   Advertising. -- (Ethical debates)
   1. Advertising--Moral and ethical aspects--
Juvenile
   literature.
   I. Title II. Series
   174.9'659-dc22
ISBN 978 0 7502 6567 6

Printed in China

Wayland is a division of
Hachette Children's Books,
an Hachette UK company.
www.hachette.co.uk

Picture acknowledgements:
The author and publisher would like to
thank the following agencies for allowing
these pictures to be reproduced:

Advertising Archives: 15, 16, 17, 23, 24, 25,
         26, 27, 28, 31, 32, 33,34, 35, 37,
         38, 41.
auremar/Shutterstock: 43.
Mathias Beinling/Alamy: 21.

Bloomberg/Getty Images: 7b.
Stu Forster/Getty Images: 19.
Kaspars Grinvalds/Shutterstock: fr. cover.
Hallgerd/istockphoto: 8.
Ho Phillip/Shutterstock: 6b.
Peter Horree/Alamy: 11, 30.
JustASC/Shutterstock: 14.
Levi's ®: 13.
Lou-Photo/Alamy: 1, 29.
MGM/EON/Kobal Collection: 40.
Chris Pancewicz/Alamy: 12.
David Parker/Alamy: 44.
Alex Segre/Alamy: 22.
Alex Smailes/Corbis: 39.
SNEHIT/Shutterstock: 9.
Sports Illustrated/Getty Images: 5b.
Justin Sullivan/Getty Images: 10.

Every attempt has been made to clear
copyright. Should there be any
inadvertent omission please apply to the
publisher for rectification.

About the Consultant: Terry Fiehn worked
as a teacher, advisory teacher and teacher
trainer for over 20 years. He is co-author
of the *This is Citizenship* series of
textbooks and has written several history
textbooks and a wide range of educational
resources.He worked on the QCDA
Citizenship assessment working party
and monitoring programme.

Note: The website addresses (URLs) included in this book
were valid at the time of going to press. However, because of
the nature of the Internet, it is possible that some addresses
may have changed, or sites may have changed or closed
down since publication. While the author and publishers
regret any inconvenience this may cause to the readers, no
responsibility for any such changes can be accepted by either
the author or the publishers.

contents

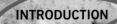

Real-life case study

This real-life case study highlights some of the issues in the debate on advertising.

case study

In 2010 the American soft drinks manufacturer Coca-Cola launched a major advertising campaign to promote its soft drink Vitaminwater in the UK. Poster ads featured a line of colourful bottled drinks with the slogan "enhanced hydration for the nation – delicious and nutritious".

However, the ad soon came under criticism. The UK advertising regulator the Advertising Standards Authority (ASA; see Chapter 6) received complaints from members of the public who maintained that Coca-Cola's claim that the product was nutritious was misleading, because the drink contained a lot of sugar.

International laws forbid advertisers to claim that their products have health benefits unless these have been proved by rigorous tests. The ASA investigated the complaints and received a statement from Coca-Cola. The company admitted that the 500-ml bottle of drink contained 23g of sugar – the same as 4-5 teaspoons. But it claimed that the drink could be called nutritious because it contained "meaningful quantities of several nutrients", including Vitamin C and four B vitamins.

In making its decision the ASA noted that a 500-ml bottle of Vitaminwater could not be considered healthy because it contained over a quarter of a person's recommended daily intake of sugar. After careful consideration, the watchdog concluded that the drink was not nutritious and banned the ad.

The 2010 ad was not the first time that the Vitaminwater range had met with criticism from the UK regulators. In 2009, a series of ads for the same brand were banned for making misleading claims about its health and nutrition benefits. One poster implied that the Power-C drink was more nutritious than vegetables, containing "More muscles than brussels". Another ad used the slogan "Keep perky when you are feeling murky". The ASA received complaints that the ads were misleading in claiming that their soft drinks would make people healthier and more resistant to disease. Coca-Cola said the ads were intended to be "humorous and irreverent" but the ASA upheld the complaints and banned the ads.

In the US in 2010, Vitaminwater also fell foul of regulators for claiming it boosted the body's immune system and reduced the risk of disease. A spokesperson for the Center for Science in the Public Interest, who sued Coca-Cola, said: "For too long, Coca-Cola has been exploiting Americans' desire to eat and drink more healthfully by deceiving them into thinking that Vitaminwater can actually prevent disease."

It's a fact

In the early 1900s, Coca-Cola ads claimed the soft drink was a health tonic that "revives and sustains", and could even cure headaches. However, by the 1920s these health claims had been dropped. Instead, Coca-Cola was presented as a drink with a fun, sporty image that would quench the nation's thirst.

▼ The information about ingredients in Vitaminwater are shown on the bottle on a partly coloured background. Some people have argued that this makes the information difficult to read.

CHAPTER 1

What is advertising?

If you live in a city, you may see more than 3,000 adverts a day, either outdoors in public spaces or indoors on TV and online. Advertising is a form of communication paid for by individuals or companies, with the aim of influencing people to think or act in a particular way or providing information. The aim of most adverts is to persuade us to buy goods or services offered by the advertiser. There are also public service adverts which convey information, and ads sponsored by charities, which encourage donations.

Advertising is a centuries-old practice, dating back to ancient Greece and Rome. It arose from a need to tell people about goods, services or events. Advertising is now a multi-million-dollar industy. Companies invest huge sums launching new products using highly sophisticated

▼ Large-scale advertising is a feature of cities around the world, such as here in Hong Kong.

techniques and persuasive language. However, a lot of advertising is designed not to promote new products but sell existing ones.

Types of advertising

We are exposed to many different forms of advertising every day. These include TV and radio commercials, newspaper or magazine ads, posters on buses, trains and buildings, and pop-ups and banner ads when surfing the Internet. Advertising may be restricted to a small, local audience, or it may be a nationwide campaign. The industry is traditionally divided into "above the line" advertising using mass media such as press, TV, radio and websites, and "below the line" advertising, targeted at individuals, for example through direct mail, mobile phones or email.

Who advertises?

Advertisers range from ordinary people and small businesses to huge multinational companies. The costs of advertising also vary vastly, from a few pounds to huge, six-figure sums. For example, for a small fee, you might place an ad in a local shop window to sell your bike or announce your services as a babysitter. On the other hand, a car manufacturer may spend many millions of pounds to advertise its latest vehicle.

Where do adverts appear?

Adverts appear in many different media, or forms of mass communication. In the advertising world these are known as channels. In the 21st century the main channels are TV and radio, the Internet, newspapers and magazines, direct mail and outdoor media, such as billboards. In addition, advertising appears in window displays, on product packaging and point of sale material in shops, and on novelty items, such as pens and key rings that are handed out for free. New or unusual channels include tickets and receipts, telesales including text messages on mobile phones, and sky writing. More recently, companies have also started advertising their products on social networking sites, such as Twitter and Facebook. They either place ads on these sites, or create company profiles and encourage people to follow them in order to receive promotions and updates on new products.

It's a fact

Over US$600 billion are now spent on advertising each year. Around half of this figure is spent in the USA. The world's two largest ad companies, Omnicom and Interpublic, are both based in New York.

YouTube, an online video platform, has become a ▶ popular advertising channel. It is accessed by millions of people worldwide daily, and videos are easy to embed in social media messages. This means that adverts on YouTube can potentially reach a huge global audience.

TV, cinema and radio

Television advertising is sold in time slots ranging from seven seconds to a minute long. Peak slots in the evening are the most expensive because audiences are largest then. Advertisers can sponsor whole programmes, which gives them longer to expose viewers to their products. TV commercials may use a storyline, mascots, words, music and song to put across the message. These ads reach huge numbers of people while they are relaxing at home, and likely to be reasonably attentive. However, people who find adverts annoying will seek distraction during commercial breaks or record programmes so they can fast-forward through the ads. This means advertisers need to work hard to grab the viewers' attention, for example using jingles and slogans. Ads shown on the big screen at cinemas, on the other hand, are viewed without distraction.

Radio advertising allows advertisers to put over their message with a storyline and music. Like TV, it is sold in time slots, usually 30 seconds or a minute long. People listen to the radio while doing other things, such as driving, so ads need to be able to draw attention. As with TV advertising, peak slots, such as rush hours, are more expensive. As there is a huge variety of stations on both a national and a regional level, advertisers are able to target particular groups and locations.

The press

Newspapers, magazines and trade directories such as Yellow Pages are all part of the press. Newspaper ads include

▼ TV advertisers select time slots to target particular audiences. Ads aimed at children are usually shown early in the morning and in the early evening.

Billboard ads in city centres or on major routes reach millions of people day and night. Often the ads merely consist of the company logo or their slogan. This is very immediate and creates an awareness of brands and products.

display ads and classified or small ads. Together these form about half the content of most newspapers. Some newspapers sell enough advertising space on their pages that they can be handed out for free. Newspaper advertising has the advantage that it can quickly respond to events, such as major news stories. Newspaper and magazine ads can express complex ideas, such as how devices work. High-quality printing in magazines allows advertisers to put across glossy images that may suggest a product is of high value. Many magazines are kept for weeks and read by several people, for instance in waiting rooms.

Direct mail
Leaflets and brochures delivered by the postal service are known as direct mail. Most direct mail is generated by mail-order companies who may do much of their business by post. Direct mail may be delivered to every household in an area, but more often it is sent to selected addresses from a mailing list. These lists are created by specialist research firms. Some lists consist of people who have responded to spam emails (see page 10) in the past, and people included on them could even be targeted by fraudsters.

Modern technologies such as the Internet and mobile phones allow advertisers to target their message at people as individuals, in order to reflect personal tastes.

The Internet

Internet advertising has grown quickly since the invention of the World Wide Web in the 1990s. Online adverts include large banners, smaller text ads and pop-ups. There are also online classifieds and ads on apps for mobile devices. In addition to having their own websites, companies place ads on search engines or social network sites, such as Facebook and Bebo. They may send emails to customers who are identified when they buy products or register guarantees online. Emails are also sent indiscriminately; these are known as spam. Spam is generally unpopular with Internet-users as it clutters up email inboxes. It also results in children seeing highly inappropriate material, for example ads selling drugs or pornography. Using social networking sites and video sharing platforms such as YouTube, companies may also conduct viral advertising campaigns. This technique involves posting Internet-exclusive material (for example a video or a game) on the Internet and spreading it via Facebook, Bebo, Myspace and other networking sites. The aim is to create brand awareness and reach as many people as possible by being recommended through social, rather than commercial channels.

A powerful influence

Advertising is everywhere, and most people accept that it is an essential part of a consumer society. Many people have strong views on advertising. Advertisers say adverts present useful information about products, giving consumers a wide range of choice. Critics say adverts aim to create needs that do not exist, and to manipulate people – to persuade us to buy things by playing on emotions such as fear and guilt. They say advertising encourages people to envy others. Some people find adverts amusing, others find them irritating or distracting. This book will explore how advertising works and the debate about its effects on society.

It's a fact

Advertising as we know it was shaped by the invention of printing in the 1400s. By the 1600s, printed handbills and notices were becoming common. In the late 1800s the Industrial Revolution led to a growth in advertising, to publicise goods that were mass-produced for the first time. In the 20th century, the arrival of radio in the 1920s and television in the 1950s created new mass audiences for advertising.

▲ Outdoor advertising is displayed on buses, overground and underground
trains, and at stations. The ad may well be seen for just a few seconds,
so the message has to be strong and fairly simple.

v i e w p o i n t s

"Advertising is totally unnecessary. Unless
you hope to make money."
Jef I. Richards (US advertising professor)

"Advertising is the art of convincing people
to spend money they don't have for
something they don't need."
Will Rogers (American entertainer, 1879-1935)

s u m m a r y

▶ Adverts are messages paid for by
advertisers to provide information
or persuade us to buy something.

▶ Adverts appear in a wide variety of
different media, including TV, radio,
the press and the Internet. These
are known as channels.

▶ Internet advertising has grown
rapidly since the early 1990s.

CHAPTER 2

Why advertise?

One of the main purposes of advertising is to sell something. Manufacturers, such as soft drinks companies, and retailers, such as DIY stores, advertise to promote their products. Organisations, such as airlines, telephone companies, banks and building societies, advertise their services.

Commercial advertising

Companies advertise for a variety of reasons, including to launch new products, increase their market share at the expense of rivals and recruit new staff. When a major company launches a new product, it is often promoted through multiple channels. In the course of a single day, you might learn of the product on the radio, at the shopping centre, on posters, TV and on the Internet. However, companies also spend a lot of money promoting existing products, to increase their share of the market. Not all advertising is aimed at the general public. Companies also advertise to recruit new staff, and to other businesses – this is called B2B (Business to Business) advertising. B2B ads are placed in specialist channels or venues, for example in trade magazines or at trade fairs, to increase sales.

Companies also advertise to improve their corporate image – to create a favourable impression with the public. Industries that may suffer from a negative image, such as oil companies and power companies using nuclear energy, spend large sums to convince us that their safety record is good or that they care about the environment.

Brand image

The key to advertising is often the creation of a successful brand image. This is the

In 2000, the international oil giant BP relaunched itself as a major investor in clean, renewable energy. The campaign included a new logo and cost over US$30 million. However, BP's clean image was badly damaged by the Gulf of Mexico oil spill in 2010.

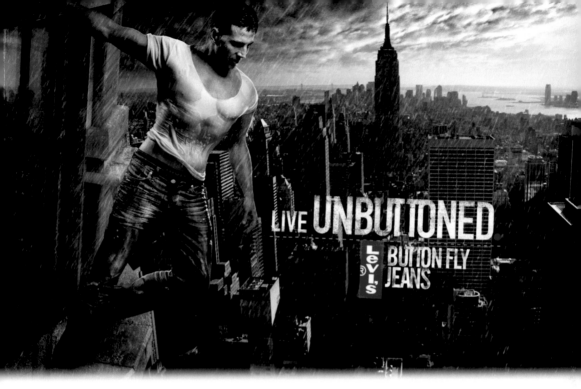

▲ Levi's Jeans adverts aim to produce a 'cool' image for the product that will appeal to young people.

image or lifestyle associated with the brand or product, such as the world of glamour and fashion, or a 'cool' image designed to appeal to young people. The image is linked to the group the advertiser hopes to target, such as male teenagers, young mothers or the over-60s. If the branding is successful, the image will eventually be conveyed through just a simple logo, such as the Nike "swoosh", or a trademark, such as Coca-Cola.

Product comparison

When trying to increase their market share, companies may directly refer to other brands and explain why the product advertised is superior. Where the product closely resembles its rivals, this technique, called product comparison, can present quite a challenge for the ad team. For example, there are hundreds of different types of toothpaste on the market. Since these products are essentially similar, many toothpaste companies successfully target their products at different groups of consumers, for example, young children, smokers or people with sensitive gums. This is called positioning. Strict rules govern adverts that compare the prices of one brand or retailer with its competitors. Such ads are required to be entirely truthful and accurate. Supermarkets and other retailers sometimes overstep the mark in trying to win customers from their rivals. In February 2011, the UK retailer Asda placed adverts offering to give customers a refund if they were able to find the same goods at cheaper prices in their competitors' stores. Rival supermarkets Morrisons and Tesco complained that Asda had not made it clear that the price guarantee only applied to grocery items. The advertising regulator, the Advertising Standards Authority investigated the complaints and decided they were valid. Asda was told to change the ads.

Government and political advertising

Governments spend large amounts on advertising. The money goes on public service ads that provide information, and also on recruitment, including to the armed forces. Political parties are major advertisers, particularly in the run-up to an election. Nowadays political advertising is highly sophisticated. Ad agencies are employed to portray party politics and candidates with a gloss or 'spin' that will appeal to voters. Ad campaigns may also aim to expose the weaknesses of rival candidates and policies. However, too much of this 'negative advertising' has been shown to put off voters. In the run-up to the UK government election in 1997, a Conservative party ad showed then Labour leader Tony Blair with demonic eyes, and the slogan "New Labour, New Danger". The ad attracted criticism that it had no real content and was just "scare-mongering".

Critics say that political advertising gives the richest parties an unfair advantage over their rivals. In countries such as the UK, political spending is tightly regulated.

It's a fact

In 2010 the British government spent £253 million on advertising – up almost 40 per cent on the previous year.

This US poster shows Uncle Sam, a character who symbolises the US government. It was based on a British poster featuring a British general, Lord Kitchener, that had the words "Your country needs you". Both posters were used to recruit soldiers for World War I.

However, in an election year out-going governments often spend large sums to advertise their records and achievements. Many people believe this is a misuse of taxpayers' money.

Public service ads

Governments around the world invest in public service ads that inform citizens about health, safety and environmental issues, such as climate change, obesity and HIV/AIDS. Ads that highlight, say, the dangers of drinking alcohol and driving, or the importance of smoke alarms in homes, often use shocking images. A drink-driving ad may feature a graphic reconstruction of an accident, while a smoke alarm ad might show someone hospitalised after a severe fire. Quite often the victims shown are children. This technique, called shock advertising, is controversial. Many people find these images upsetting. Governments say they are justified to change people's behaviour.

case study

In 2007 the British government launched an anti-smoking campaign "Get Unhooked" to highlight the addictive nature of smoking. Over five weeks, ads in the press, on TV and on the Internet showed smokers with large fishhooks piercing their lips or cheeks as a way of illustrating how people get "hooked" on cigarettes.

Many viewers found the ads upsetting. The Advertising Standards Agency (ASA), which regulates British advertising (see Chapter 6), received over 770 complaints about the campaign – the most for several years. The regulator upheld the complaints, forcing the government to withdraw the ads from television on the grounds that they were likely to "frighten and distress children". However, the press and Internet campaign was allowed to continue. A government spokesperson said the campaign had been "highly effective" in putting across the addictive nature of smoking. A quit-smoking helpline and website had been contacted a record 820,000 times during the campaign.

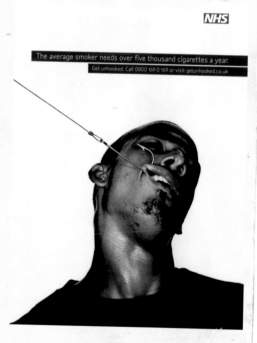

The average smoker needs over five thousand cigarettes a year.
Get unhooked. Call 0800 169 0 169 or visit getunhooked.co.uk

NHS

▲ The 2007 "Get Unhooked" anti-smoking campaign was launched ahead of a ban on smoking in public places, which took effect that year.

Charity advertising

Many charities spend heavily on advertising. Aid organisations such as Oxfam and Save the Children advertise to raise awareness of issues including poverty and hunger. Animal charities such as the RSPCA and pressure groups such as Greenpeace advertise to highlight animal rights or environmental issues. Such campaigns aim to win support and donations, which will allow their work to continue.

As with public service ads, charity ads quite often use distressing or shocking images. For example, aid agencies may show sick

case study

Shock advertising

In 2008, the UK children's charity Barnardo's launched a campaign to highlight the problem of child abuse. A 60-second TV ad showed scenes in which a teenage girl was beaten up and eventually took illegal drugs. The scenes were then repeated several times in quick succession. The message was: "For thousands of children in the UK the story will keep repeating itself, until someone stops it". Many people, including survivors of child abuse, found the ad extremely upsetting. Many felt it was unsuitable to be seen by children. The ASA received over 840 complaints. After careful consideration, the regulator decided not to uphold the complaints, because "Even though it could be seen as shocking, the aim of the ad justified the use of such strong imagery." After the decision the ASA continued to receive complaints, suggesting that the campaign may have cost Barnardo's considerable support.

▲ A still from the Barnardo's ad that raised a storm of protest. The controversy over the ad generated further publicity for the charity, creating awareness of their work, but possibly also damaging their image with potential supporters.

It takes up to 40 dumb animals to make a fur coat.

But only one to wear it.

LYNX
Fighting the fur trade

If you don't want animals gassed, electrocuted, trapped or strangled, don't buy a fur coat. P O Box 509 Dunmow, Essex Tel: 0371 2016

◀ This Lynx ad, which incorporated an image by top photographer David Bailey, was widely admired for its effectiveness in putting across a hard-hitting message.

or starving children in regions such as Africa, coupled with an appeal for money. Critics say such ads portray people in less developed countries as helpless victims, reliant on Western aid. They say that the images are designed to guilt-trip us into giving money. Some aid organisations reply that such images are justified to arouse people's sympathy and raise money for a good cause. However, many have taken the criticism on board and try to present more positive images in their adverts, for example Africans using development money to improve their own resources.

Designed to shock

Animal charities and environmental pressure groups may also use shock advertising to stress the need for people to support their cause. For example, the animal charity the Brooke Foundation has used images of donkeys collapsed under heavy loads to raise money for animal welfare. In the 1980s, the animal rights group Lynx launched a campaign against the fur trade. A famous image (see above) showed a glamorous female model dragging a fur coat dripping blood. The slogan was "It takes up to 40 dumb animals to make a fur coat. But only one to wear

it." The ad was criticised for being offensive to women. Lynx countered by saying that the ad showed "the unpleasant reality behind the glamorous image portrayed by the fur industry". The campaign won massive public support. People stopped buying fur coats, and fur sales in the UK dropped by 50 per cent. A recent ad by the charity PETA is even more hard-hitting. Under the heading "Here's the rest of your fur coat", celebrities such as Sophie Ellis-Bextor hold the carcass of a skinned animal up to the viewer.

summary

▶ Commercial businesses, political parties, governments and charities are all major advertisers.

▶ Governments use public service ads to raise awareness about health and safety issues. Political parties advertise heavily during election campaigns.

▶ Companies, governments and charities sometimes use upsetting images to put across their message.

CHAPTER 3

The business of advertising

Advertising is big business. When a company decides to advertise a product, it engages an advertising company. The ad company acts as a link between the client and the creative team who put the ad together. The client briefs the ad company on the aim of the campaign. The two then liaise to define the message. They must also decide which media to use. Channels such as the press and Internet sites submit figures on circulation and users to help make this decision.

Target audiences

A key part of devising an ad campaign is determining the target audience – the group of consumers who are most likely to buy the product. This will affect the branding strategy – how the product is packaged and advertised. Market research helps to define the target group. The study of social groups is called demographics. Social groups are generally defined by profession, age, social status and at a more detailed level, by where people live. These social groupings are generally taken as an indication of spending power. After careful consideration, an advertiser may decide to target a broad grouping, for example, women aged between 20 and 50, or a much narrower audience, such as white males from group B (see table below) aged 35-45, living in north London.

Repositioning

The aiming of a product at a particular group of consumers is called positioning. Over time, if a company decides it wants to target a different group, it will change the product's brand image. This is called repositioning. A classic example occurred in the 1950s. The cigarette manufacturer Marlboro decided it wanted to retarget its filter cigarettes, which were mainly smoked by women, at men. The ad company came up with the idea of a cowboy as an ultra-masculine image that would appeal to men. A cigarette-smoking cowboy became the focus of a long-running campaign which successfully sold the brand to men and resulted in a 300 per cent increase in sales in just two years. Later, when the harmful effects of smoking were known, cigarette advertisers had to cope with increasing restrictions and were legally bound to print government health warnings both on printed ads and on cigarette packaging.

▼ This table shows a system commonly used in the advertising industry of grouping people by occupation.

Group	Occupation
A	Higher managerial, administrative and professional
B	Intermediate managerial, administrative and professional
C1	Supervisory / clerical and junior managerial, administrative and professional
C2	Skilled manual
D	Semi-skilled and unskilled manual
E	Casual labourers, state pensioners and the unemployed

Source: Advertising Association

case study

Repositioning Lucozade

Lucozade is an energy drink made in the UK. It was created in 1927 for people suffering from minor illnesses, such as colds. For decades, the drink was marketed as a tonic with the slogan "Lucozade aids recovery". In 1983 the manufacturers GlaxoSmithKline hired the ad company Ogilvy & Mather to boost flagging sales.

The team suggested energy drink, associated with sport and fitness. A series of ads featured Olympic athletes, with a new slogan "Lucozade replaces lost energy". The effects were dramatic: UK sales tripled in five years. Nowadays food and drink manufacturers have to be very careful in making any claims about the health benefits of their products, and back up any claims with hard evidence.

▼ Lucozade advertises at a wide variety of sporting events, such as London Marathon, shown here.

Advertising is one of the world's leading industries. It generates huge revenues for governments in taxes and creates hundreds of thousands of jobs worldwide. The USA is the world's largest advertiser; Germany, Japan and the UK are also major players. One to two per cent of all income in the UK is spent on advertising. Advertising can help economies to grow by stimulating the demand for products.

However, advertising aimed at encouraging consumers to switch from one brand to another has little effect on the economy.

Funding the media

Advertising largely pays for newspapers and magazines, allowing for free circulation in some cases. It also funds commercial TV and radio stations, and Internet sites such as YouTube, Google and Facebook.

The headquarters of Interpublic in New York City, USA. Interpublic is one of the world's largest advertising companies. In the first decade of the 21st century the ten biggest ad companies were all based in more economically developed countries, such as the USA, the UK, France and Japan.

An increasing number of TV programmes and films are also sponsored by advertising, as are major sporting events. Without advertising, many of these media would not exist, and the sporting calendar would look very different. Large sporting events, such as the Olympics, receive significant funds through advertising, and professional sportspeople often have sponsorship deals by which they receive funding in return for advertising their sponsor.

Many people believe that advertising influences the content of the media. For example, research has shown that newspapers and magazines sponsored by alcohol advertisers are less likely to run articles on the harmful effects of alcohol. On TV, as advertising has grown, so programming on commercial channels has become less geared towards education, and more towards entertainment. Many people believe that this is because of pressure from advertisers, who prefer entertainment programmes since they provide larger audiences, thus giving advertisers better value for money.

However, few TV companies are willing to admit that they allow advertising to affect programming.

Advertising and prices

The cost of advertising a product is nearly always included in the price charged to consumers. The percentage of the unit cost made up by advertising is called the advertising to sales ratio. In some cases this is relatively low, less than 5 per cent, but in products such as cosmetics and shampoo it may be over 30 per cent.

Experts disagree on the overall effect that advertising has on the prices consumers pay for goods. Some experts maintain that the huge sums spent on advertising increase the price of many goods, since the costs of advertising are included in the unit price and so passed on to customers. Manufacturers counter this by arguing that advertising increases sales, which allows them to mass-produce goods. This lowers the unit price, and the savings can then be passed onto the consumer. In addition, many companies regularly offer goods at reduced prices to increase sales.

▼ This chart shows the top ten global media spenders in 2009. The ten highest spenders are all based in the USA, Europe or Japan.

Company	Total spent on advertising in 2009
1. Procter and Gamble Co.	US$8.68 billion
2. Unilever	US$6.03 billion
3. L'Oréal	US$4.56 billion
4. General Motors Co.	US$3.27 billion
5. Nestlé	US$2.62 billion
6. Coca-Cola Co.	US$2.44 billion
7. Toyota Motor Corp.	US$2.31 billion
8. Johnson & Johnson	US$2.25 billion
9. Reckitt Benckiser	US$2.24 billion
10. Kraft Foods	US$2.12 billion

summary

▶ Companies engage advertising agencies to research and put together ad campaigns.

▶ The target audience at which the product is aimed affects the way it is marketed.

▶ Advertising is a major industry, creating enormous wealth and employing hundreds of thousands of people.

CHAPTER 4

How do adverts work?

To be effective, advertising has to influence the way we think or behave. Ads use many different tricks and techniques to do this. In 1957, a book called *The Hidden Persuaders* by Vance Packard claimed that advertisers use psychological techniques to persuade people to buy. Most advertisers acknowledge they aim to manipulate our emotions. Some people feel that at its most extreme, advertising is a form of brain-washing.

In the early days of advertising, most ads were a simple and straightforward appeal to buy the product. This technique, called a "hard sell", is still widely used, for example when a sale is announced with the appeal to "Buy now, while stocks last". However, many ads are now extremely subtle. They may tell a complex story without even mentioning the product, or keep its identity a mystery until the very end. This has the effect of arousing our curiosity, which is a classic advertising technique.

A technique called subliminal advertising involves messages flashed so briefly on a TV, cinema or computer screen that we are not aware of them. This technique aims to make us subconsciously familiar with a product, so we are more likely to buy it when we see it in shops. Subliminal advertising is highly controversial. Many people see it as extremely manipulative and it is now banned in many countries. However, advertisers point out that its effectiveness has never been proved.

An example of "hard sell" advertising – a simple announcement of a sale. This type of advertising uses a straightforward and overt message. The product or brand is clearly identified from the start.

viewpoints

"Advertising is legalised lying."
H. G. Wells, English writer

"Advertisements contain the only truths to be relied on in a newspaper."
US writer Mark Twain

case study

A classic ad

In 1999, the drinks manufacturer Diageo commissioned a 60-second TV commercial to sell Guinness stout. Filmed in black-and-white, the ad opens with a closeup of a Polynesian man's face. The voiceover speaks about waiting. We realise the man is one of a group of surfers who are waiting for perfect surf conditions. When the surf is up, the men run down to the sea and paddle out. Computer graphics turn the foaming waves into white horses with tossing manes. Haunting drum music is heard as a voice murmurs: "the old sailors return to the bar..." Viewers may well be enjoying the advert while wondering what it is about.

The surfers are menaced by the flailing hooves of the wave-horses. One by one they capsize. The drumming becomes louder and we hear the sound of someone smacking his lips after slaking his thirst. The remaining lone surfer makes it to the shore and the others greet him as a hero. We cut abruptly to the image of a pint of foaming Guinness with the voiceover "Here's to waiting." A headline on the screen reads: "Good things come to those who...".

The Guinness "surfer" campaign cost US$6 million. The ad won many awards, and still regularly tops UK viewers' polls of the best advert of all time. It is a classic example of a technique called a "soft sell" – subtly selling the product by creating an image or a "feel" to the product, rather than explicitly stating what the benefits are of using or consuming it. Here, the identity of the product is not even revealed until the last seconds, keeping the audience guessing and making the final punchline all the more effective.

▲ This scene in the Guinness ad was inspired by a painting by UK artist Walter Crane called "Neptune's Horses". Painted in 1893, it showed a line of white horses galloping along a cresting wave.

Advertising techniques

Most ads follow the advertising principle AIDA, which stands for Attract, Interest, Desire, Action. An ad must first attract our attention and arouse interest. It must then generate desire for the product or service, and finally prompt action – normally to buy, or give money in the case of charities. Leading US ad executive Leo Burnett said: "Advertising says to people, 'Here's what we've got. Here's what it will do for you. Here's how to get it.'"

Print, poster and Internet ads use images, colours, words and design to sell products. The headline grabs our attention while the slogan sums up the message. Slogans such as Nike's "Just do it" are designed to stick in the mind. The company's logo often features prominently to help us recognise the brand. TV, radio and film ads use moving images to draw viewers in, entertain them and present reasons for buying. These ads also use music to hold our attention. The slogan is often set to music, becoming a catchy jingle. Some ads use extended storylines that unfold over a whole series of ads, creating a soap opera effect. People are more likely to watch these ads because they want to follow the storyline.

Ads in all channels use repetition to drive home their message. The slogan and logo may appear several times in a single ad, and the ad itself may also be repeated – either in a series of posters or by being aired many times a week.

Singer, songwriter and actress Beyoncé Knowles is among a host of celebrities used by the cosmetics company L'Oréal to lend glamour to their products. The French company is one of the world's largest advertisers. However, by law a celebrity must actually use a product if they say they do.

Endorsements

A common advertising technique that has been used for centuries is the appeal to authority. Dentists or actors posing as dentists recommend toothpaste. Doctors endorse all sorts of health products. In the mid-1900s, they were even used to endorse cigarettes – a practice which was outlawed once the harmful effects of smoking were known. Images of white-coated scientists are used to promote a huge range of products, from skin creams to washing powder. The aim is to reassure us that the product is safe and has been thoroughly "tried and tested". However, consumers are not always aware that the "experts" are often just actors.

case study

Testimonials

Celebrities from the world of sport, film, TV and media have been used to sell products since the 1800s. Such ads are called "testimonials". The celebrity may be connected with the product sold, for example a motor racing star may endorse a car, but quite often the star and product are unconnected. Young, attractive sports stars are in great demand for advertising. Many sports celebrities earn huge sums from advertising. However, campaigns involving sports stars can backfire, for example if an advertiser hires an athlete to coincide with the start of a major competition, only to see the star knocked out at an early stage.

In the mid-1900s, cigarette ▶ manufacturers such as Camel tried to sell their product using reassuring authority figures such as doctors. The text claimed research showed this brand was popular among doctors without saying how many doctors were interviewed. Once the harmful effects of smoking were known, cigarettes were no longer associated with the medical profession. Smoking was more generally associated with being manly, hip or cool. Now cigarette advertising is severely restricted in most countries.

Dispelling suspicion

Humour is often used in advertising. It has the effect of dispelling viewers' suspicions. If we are amused by an ad, we are more likely to buy the product, and the ad may even become a talking point. Another technique advertisers use to disarm us is to show "real" people, such as DIY store assistants or bank staff, selling products or services – even though the "real" people are often actors.

Dreams, desires and fears

Many ads work by appealing to guilt or common needs and desires, for example the desire to be attractive, popular and successful. A shampoo ad featuring a beautiful model suggests the product will make you more attractive. A jeans ad showing cool teenagers having a good time suggests the brand will make you popular. In 1985, a Levi's ad showing a young man stripping in a laundromat

◀ This ad for Kerrygold butter suggests the product contains no additives at all, even though it does contain salt. Ads for dairy products or margarine are often located in idealised countryside settings, such as meadows with mooing cows or rustic breakfast tables. Such images aim to suggest that the products contain only natural ingredients, which may not be the case.

to wash his 501 jeans implied the product conferred sex appeal. The Cadbury's Flake ads of the 1970s involving glamorous models gave chocolate a new, sexy image. One ad was banned following complaints it was suggestive. Some advertisers openly acknowledge that they aim to manipulate us in this way. For example, Charles Revson, who founded Revlon Cosmetics, said "In our factory, we make lipstick. In our advertising, we sell hope." Critics say such appeals are exploitative and underhand.

Many ads set out to sell a product by evoking an attractive or glamorous lifestyle, such as the sun-drenched Caribbean or the world of spies and fast cars. The Guinness ad on page 23 was set in the glamorous world of surfing. It also told of success against the odds. The flipside of this technique is ads that play on our fears, rather than desires. We have already seen how governments and charities often use shock tactics to put across a message. This technique is also known as "scare and sell".

case study

Using nostalgia

Nostalgia (thinking fondly about the past) is often used to sell products. The UK company Premier Foods created a popular brand image for Hovis bread with a series of ads that evoked life in Britain in the mid-1900s, with cobbled streets and brass band music. The ads aimed to suggest that Hovis was wholesome and traditional. Other ads that play on sentiment often use cosy images of parents or grandparents playing with young children.

▲ Hovis ads imply the bread is baked according to a tried and tested traditional recipe and contains only healthy ingredients, without actually saying so. It also conveys childhood nostalgia, aiming to evoke strong emotional responses from viewers.

New Nurofen Long Lasting can give period pain the push for up to 12 hours.

For effective relief from period pain reach for new Nurofen Long Lasting. One dose of the unique controlled-release formulation can help alleviate pain for up to 12 hours. Leaving you to concentrate on the more important things in life. Available from your pharmacist.

Works at the site of pain for up to 12 hours.

new NUROFEN long lasting

12 Targeted relief for pain

Contains ibuprofen. Always read the label. www.nurofen.com

◀ Manufacturers of painkillers sometimes use semi-scientific jargon to sell the product. They may claim the product "works up to three times faster" or lasts longer. But faster and longer than what? And "up to" provides a further get-out clause.

Product comparison

Every product that sells well has a "Unique Selling Proposition", or USP for short. This is a quality that sets it apart from others. In the case of products such as shampoo, where brands are essentially similar, brand image often provides the USP. For example, there are hundreds of skin creams on the market, differing widely in price. Low-price products are targeted at customers seeking value for money, while expensive ones are sold as luxury items that will "pamper your skin".

The language of advertising

By law, advertisers are forbidden to say anything they know to be false. However, carefully chosen language can be used to mislead us. Critics call such language "weasel words" and say their aim is to deceive. Many ads use words such as "helps to", "virtually" and "often" to avoid promising anything definite. For example, an advertiser may claim a cleaning product "helps to combat dirt" or "gets surfaces virtually spotless". "Helps to" and "virtually" gets the advertiser out of claiming something that could be shown as false. Pseudo-scientific language such as "new, improved formula" and "laboratory tested" are commonly used. So are vague statistics, such as "Seventy per cent of users say…" without saying how many people were asked. TV ads show the amount of people asked in surveys, but usually in small print and for short amount of time. This means that the information can easily be missed by the viewer.

▲ The sportswear manufacturer Nike is so successful that the Nike logo or
"swoosh" is a USP in its own right. In a brand-conscious world, many people
are prepared to pay considerably more for a branded product than a less
familiar brand.

Decoding advertisements

Advertisers say they have a right to free
speech. Consumer groups say advertisers
have a duty to deal honestly with the
public. Consumer Education UK warns:
"Advertising will only ever tell half the story
– the half the advertiser wants you to
know." But just as adverts are put together
by an ad team, so we can unpick or decode
them. Look critically at a couple of adverts
in different media. Who do you think the
ad is aimed at? Does it play on emotions,
such as the desire to be popular or the fear
of rejection? Is the USP something definite,
or is it just hype?

It's a fact

The idea of USP was invented by US ad
executive Rosser Reeves in the 1940s.
Reeves explained: "Every advertisement
must say to each reader, 'Buy this product
and you will get this specific benefit: one
that the competition either cannot, or does
not, offer'".

summary

▶ Adverts use the principle AIDA,
which stands for Attention, Interest,
Desire, Action.

▶ Many ads use endorsements from
celebrities or authority figures,
such as doctors and scientists,
to persuade us to buy.

▶ Many ads work by appealing to
people's deep-seated needs or
common fears.

CHAPTER 5

Advertising and society

Advertising is a powerful force in society. Advertisers are always out to generate "media chatter" – to get people talking about their product. Slogans and jingles become part of everyday speech. Many people believe that advertising can affect or even create social trends, particularly among young people. Advertisers say they provide information that benefits consumers. They say that many people enjoy ads. Critics say advertising can have a harmful effect on society and people's values.

Need and greed

Advertising is widely criticised for encouraging people to become greedy and materialistic. Some experts say it makes us want things we don't need and may not be able to afford. This can lead to waste and even encourage people to get into debt. Advertisers reply that ads reflect the materialistic world we live in, not create it. Some people feel that ads can even be dangerous. For example, ads for cosmetics and clothes are marketed using slim, youthful models. They may suggest, openly or subtly, that having wrinkles or a rounded stomach makes you unattractive and less popular in social circles. Ads that equate beauty with slimness may increase the number of people who suffer from health problems such as anorexia.

▼ Critics of advertising maintain that the overuse of ultraslim models in advertising may well increase the number of young people, especially girls, suffering from eating disorders such as anorexia.

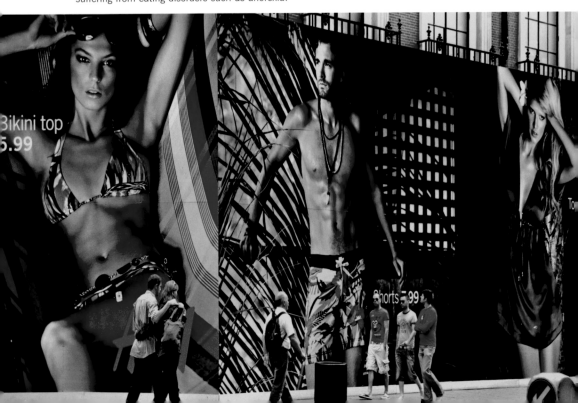

Bikini top
5.99

Shorts 5.99

To

He wears the cleanest shirts in town

...his "Missus" swears by TIDE

He wears the cleanest shirts in town!
There isn't any doubt
That all his shirts are washed with TIDE
'Cause when TIDE's in ... dirt's out!

▲ For decades, feminist groups have complained that washing powder ads represent women as domesticated creatures whose chief concern is the whiteness of their wash.

case study

Stereotyping

Many people are concerned about the use of stereotypes in advertising. A stereotype is a standardised and over-simplified image of a particular group, such as the fussy mother-in-law or the hen-pecked husband. There are also racial stereotypes, such as the lager-drinking Australian or etiquette-conscious Japanese. Advertisers say they use stereotypes because they provide a quick way of getting a point across, which is essential in a short TV commercial or on a billboard that will only be seen for seconds. Critics say that using stereotypes can lead to prejudice. They also point out that ads present a vision of the world which suggests that to get on in life, you need to be white, well-off and good-looking. Groups such as black and Asian people are under-represented in advertising. For example, Asians form four per cent of the UK population, but are rarely shown in ads.

Children and advertising

Many people are particularly concerned about the effects of advertising on young people. Research shows that children are very susceptible (open) to advertising. The average child in the UK, USA or Australia may see 30,000 adverts in a year, and even very young children absorb slogans, jingles and logos. The UK research group Compass concluded in a 2006 report: "The impact of the consumer society is now so deep that seven out of ten three-year-olds recognise the McDonald's logo, but only half know their own surname".

Ads for children's toys and games often make use of cartoon characters, bright colours and magical settings because advertisers know these will appeal to the target group. Young children generally lack the experience and critical skills to understand the tricks used by advertisers, or even that a product is being sold. Advertising to young children is highly controversial, and in many countries it is carefully controlled (see Chapter 6).

Teenagers

Many people feel that even older children are open to being manipulated by advertising, including via online social networking sites. Ads aimed at teenagers often play on the fears and insecurities that are common among young people, for example the desire to be popular, look attractive and be part of a group. Companies selling products from jeans and soft drinks to banking services target teenagers relentlessly in an effort to get them buying their brand or service. This is because research has shown that once brand loyalty is established it can last for years.

▼ A 2009 Nintendo Wii TV ad for "Mario and Sonic at the Olympic Winter Games". Console games that are advertised to children often include cartoon-style characters or mascots that are believed to increase the appeal of the product.

Some people worry that fast food ads encourage children and adults to develop a poor diet, which contains a lot of fatty or sugary foods.

Supporters of advertising say that it helps young people learn how things work in our consumer-led society. They say that exposure to ads can help children to become more critical and selective. Others say that young people should be shielded against the most persuasive forms of advertising, such as ads that play on fears and anxieties. They say that ads that equate success or popularity with buying the right brand encourage young people to be selfish and materialistic. Stereotyped images of beauty may have a harmful impact on young people, especially girls, leading to eating disorders. At the other extreme, fast food advertising can encourage children to develop poor dietary habits that can lead to obesity, either in their teenage years or later in life.

viewpoints

"Kids are the most pure consumers you could have. They tend to interpret your ad literally. They are infinitely open."
Debra McMahon, vice-president of US consultancy firm Mercer Management Consulting

"Our children would find it a lot easier to make healthy food choices if advertising wasn't pulling them in the opposite direction."
Kaye Mehta, Coalition on Food Advertising to Children

summary

▶ Some people believe that advertising can make people greedy and materialistic.

▶ Many ads use stereotypes to put across their message, and act to reinforce stereotypes.

▶ Many people worry that children are especially vulnerable to the techniques of advertising.

CHAPTER 6

Checks and controls

The persuasive power of advertising is generally accepted. For this reason, many countries across the world have laws to control advertising. The industry itself has organisations which publish codes of conduct. Responsible advertisers feel it is in their interest that the industry is properly regulated, so that claims made by advertisers can be believed.

Advertising and the law

In the UK, one of the main laws governing advertising is the Trade Descriptions Act. This states that advertisers must not make false claims about the products or services they advertise. The Consumer Protection Act covers ads for sales and bargains, including on the Internet.

The Broadcasting Act of 1990 covers TV and radio advertising. Other laws cover discrimination on grounds of race, sex and against people with disabilities. In 2000, the sportswear giant Nike had to withdraw an ad after complaints about the way it portrayed disabled people. Similar laws exist in America, Australia, across the European Union and in most nations around the world.

Some advertisers believe that the laws governing the industry are too restrictive. Critics, on the other hand, believe the laws need to be extended and made tighter, especially in the case of Internet advertising, as children are more likely to be exposed to unsuitable ads here.

▼ In 1992, the Italian clothes company Benetton offended some people with this ad showing a naked newborn baby. Others felt the ad reflected life and was not offensive.

UNITED COLORS OF BENETTON.

◄ In 1998, the soft drink Sunny Delight was launched in the UK as a vitamin-rich drink for children. However, tests later showed it contained only five per cent fruit juice and a lot of sugar. Reports that a child had turned orange after drinking it made sales plummet. The product had to be relaunched in 2002 under the new brand SunnyD.

case study

A question of belief?

Adverts that promote goods or services that are controversial can spark a storm of debate by their very nature. In 2010, the charity Marie Stopes, which offers sexual and reproductive healthcare services, launched the first ever UK TV ads to promote pregnancy advice. Three ads featured women who had missed their periods, with a voiceover promoting Marie Stopes as a source of advice.

The ads provoked thousands of complaints before they even went on air. The campaign became no 7 in the list of UK ads that have attracted the most complaints. Objectors said they offended many people's religious beliefs, trivialised the decision to have an abortion, and would encourage young people to be promiscuous. The ASA investigated the complaints but found that the ads were not offensive, did not trivialise the issue and did not encourage promiscuity. The complaints were not upheld.

Dangerous substances

The advertising of dangerous substances such as tobacco and alcohol is tightly controlled in most nations. However, laws vary from country to country. In the US, tobacco advertising has been banned on TV and radio since 1971, but it is allowed in other media, provided that ads include a government health warning. Advertising alcohol is only allowed in media that will reach mainly adults. Advertising contraceptives, gambling and firearms is not allowed on network TV, but permitted on some cable channels. In the UK it is illegal to advertise tobacco, guns, gambling and contraceptives. However, it is legal for the UK government to advertise to promote the use of contraceptives. Alcohol advertising is legal within certain guidelines. Advertising contraceptives is lawful in some European countries, such as Germany. In all of these countries there are people who believe the rules should be extended to cover products such as slimming pills and even fatty foods and sugary drinks.

Advertising watchdogs

Almost every country has 'watchdogs' within the advertising industry that make sure standards are maintained. In the US, regulators include the American Advertising Federation (AAF) and the Federal Trade Commission (FTC). Australian watchdogs include the Advertising Federation of Australia. In the UK it's the Advertising Standards Authority (ASA), while Ofcom regulates TV, radio and telecommunications. There are also consumer groups such as Consumer Education UK, and consumer programmes on TV.

Advertising codes

Each of these organisations has a code of conduct which lays down guidelines for the industry. Adverts must be legal, honest and truthful. They must not be misleading. If people feel an advert breaks the code, they may file a complaint. The watchdog then investigates. If it upholds (agrees with) the complaints, the ad must be changed or withdrawn. In some cases the advertiser has to make a public apology or publish the correct information. However, sometimes if an ad has to be withdrawn it generates further publicity for the company. Unscrupulous advertisers may take advantage of this to gain extra publicity.

In 2006 the British charity Save the Children attracted complaints after launching a direct-mail campaign which aimed to highlight the high number of deaths among children in less developed regions, such as Africa, compared to children in more developed regions. The mailing featured a close-up of the eyes of an African child with the text: "If you have brown eyes, you're more likely to die young." People complained to the watchdog that the ad could be frightening to children. After considering the issue carefully, the ASA upheld the complaint on the grounds that the ad "could cause fear and distress to young children who saw it". Save the Children apologised and offered to amend the mailing if they decided to reuse it, and the ASA welcomed their response.

It's a fact

In 2008 the ASA received 26,000 complaints. It investigated all the ads that seemed to breach the rules. As a result, nearly 2,500 ads had to be altered or withdrawn.

American Advertising Federation Ethics and Principles

- Advertising shall tell the truth, and shall reveal significant facts, the omission of which would mislead the public. Advertising claims shall be substantiated [backed] by evidence.

- Advertising shall not make false, misleading, or unsubstantiated statements or claims about a competitor or his/her products or services.

- Advertising shall avoid price claims which are false or misleading, or saving claims which do not offer provable savings.

- Advertising containing testimonials shall be limited to those of competent witnesses who are reflecting a real and honest opinion or experience.

- Advertising shall be free of statements, illustrations or implications which are offensive to good taste or public decency.

case study

British Heart Foundation

The British Heart Foundation campaigns to raise awareness about the damage a poor diet can do to your heart. In 2006 it published a poster showing a young girl drinking directly from a large bottle of cooking oil, with oil spilling down her chin, to highlight the danger of eating fatty foods. The headline read: "What goes into crisps goes into you." The ASA investigated after receiving complaints from people who found the ad offensive, and were worried that children might copy this behaviour.

However, the ASA decided the latter was unlikely, and did not ask BHF to withdraw the ad. The ASA says: "There is an unwritten, but generally accepted, rule that charities are allowed slightly more leeway than other advertisers because of what they are trying to achieve. ... It would be one thing for a children's charity to use stark, violent imagery to raise awareness of child abuse and a completely different one if, for example, a fashion retailer decided to use a similar image."

What goes into crisps goes into you.

Some crisps contain 33% cooking oil. bhf.org.uk

British Heart Foundation

◀ Some people found this British Heart Foundation advert disturbing, but because the ad was "in a good cause" the ASA did not ask for it to be withdrawn.

▲ Many people believe that fast food advertising encourages children to develop a taste for fatty and sugary foods.

Regulating advertising for children

Ads aimed at children are more tightly regulated than those for the general public. TV advertising is very carefully controlled because of the influence TV has over children. In many countries, special restrictions apply to TV commercials shown in children's viewing hours. In the UK, certain ads may only be shown after 7.30pm when young children have gone to bed. The rules are further relaxed after 9pm – a time known as the watershed.

Some people believe that adverts for fast foods and snack bars should not be shown during children's television. In Australia, a group called the Coalition on Food Advertising to Children has called for all food ads to be banned during children's TV. Research has shown that a third of all ads on Australian children's TV were for food, including a great many products that were high in fat, sugar or salt, all of which are bad for health. In the US, advertising medicines and drugs during children's TV is banned. In 2003, an ad for acne treatment was withdrawn after complaints that it breached this code.

In Britain, the ASA warns: "Advertisers should take particular care when targeting their messages that children are not exposed to anything that might be harmful or upsetting."

case study

Christmas wish list

In 2006, the American retailer Wal-Mart drew widespread criticism from consumer groups by publishing a wish list for children on its website Toyland. Children were asked to choose their favourites from a range of toys passing on a conveyer belt. They were then asked to enter their parents' email address, allowing Wal-Mart to "help pester your parents". A consumer group said the retailer was "actively encouraging kids to nag for their holiday gifts". Wal-Mart responded: "Kids have been writing lists for Christmas presents for hundreds of years. All we've done is put a modern slant on the tradition".

▼ A child inspects the range of toys on sale in a Wal-Mart store in the UK. Toy companies use colourful packaging to make products more appealing to children.

summary

▶ Every country has laws that regulate advertising.

▶ The advertising industry has a voluntary code of conduct that helps to maintain standards.

▶ Ads targeted at children are checked carefully to make sure they are not harmful.

CHAPTER 7

The future of advertising: the ongoing debates

In the 1960s, the thinker Marshall McLuhan called advertising "the greatest art form of the 20th century". In the last 50 years or so, the amount of advertising has increased enormously. In future, this trend can only continue, but is advertising helpful or harmful to society?

Growth areas in advertising

The last 20–30 years have seen huge growth in advertising, and the birth of many new channels. In the UK, sponsorship of TV programmes has increased. Product placement – showing branded goods in films, cartoons and TV shows – has also grown, and generates huge sums for film- and programme-makers. In 2002, 20 advertisers,

including British Airways, Ford, Kodak, Sony and Revlon, paid a total sum of US$70 million to advertise their products in the James Bond film *Die Another Day*.

◀ The 2002 James Bond film *Die Another Day* starring Pierce Brosnan broke all records for the total spent by advertisers on product placement. Critics claimed the famous spy now had "license to shill".

◀ In the first decade of the 21st century, the American and now international restaurant chain Pizza Hut pioneered advertising in space. In 2001 they became the first company to deliver fast food in space when their vacuum-sealed pizzas arrived at the International Space Station. They have also used product placement on space missions to advertise their products on TV.

Ads have even appeared in space – in 2000, the fast-food chain Pizza Hut paid about US$1million to display their logo on a Russian rocket, whose launch was watched by millions on TV.

The fastest growing sector of the industry is online advertising. Internet downloads, including of apps (applications) are part of this. When customers download a free version of an app for a mobile device, it usually contains ads which are shown every time the download is used. The only way to get rid of the ads is to buy the full version of the app. Similar strings are attached to the downloading of programmes from commercial TV stations. Social networking sites such as Twitter are extensively used for advertising. For example in 2010, car manufacturer Range Rover recruited 40 celebrities to "tweet" about its new product, the Evoque. The company also created a new Apple iPhone app that allowed downloaders to use GPS tracking to record their journeys, which they could then share with friends via Twitter and Facebook.

Many people are irritated by online advertising, such as pop-ups, banner ads and "roadblocks" – full-screen ads that users must pass to reach a chosen site. Many web-users find flashing banners distracting. Some ads are designed to resemble error messages from operating systems, which users can find worrying. In addition, some ads lead to sites with harmful virus software or adult material that is unsuitable for children.

Most email users regularly encounter spam. The global Internet company AOL reports that up to 30 per cent of all emails sent daily are spam, which most users find invasive and annoying, and can cause computer crashes.

It's a fact

In 1995 advertisers spent US$50 million on online advertising. By 1996 the figure had reached US$200 million. In 2010 it was US$23.6 billion.

Interactive advertising

The most sophisticated forms of online advertising are interactive sites which allow companies to tailor advertising to individuals, based on information we give them. This happens through cookies. These are small files which web publishers programme to be saved onto personal computers. The file then enables advertisers to know the sites you visit, the ads you have seen, and your response.

Search engines such as Google and AOL use cookies to record users' searches. Lists of consumers may then be sold to advertisers without users' knowledge or consent. Many people feel this is an invasion of privacy. The practice attracts criticism particularly in the context of advertising aimed at young people, who may not understand how advertising works or even be aware that a product is being advertised.

Cookies are also used to target users of social networking sites, such as Facebook, Bebo and Myspace. Gathering information about users' tastes and preferences through cookies allows advertisers to place ads geared at users' interests, alongside personal messages. People are far more likely to buy a product that appears to be linked with a message from a friend, so this form of advertising can be very persuasive. Some Internet providers automatically block cookies or allow users to reject them.

In the late 1990s, the American online retailer Amazon.com became one of the first companies to target individual customers through interactive advertising. When customers select an item online, the site instantly offers more choices: "Customers who bought this also bought these…". The site includes a wish list which the user can opt to be kept private or allow friends to access. Amazon also invites customer feedback on items purchased, which may then be used to endorse the product.

Information gathering

Every time you browse commercial sites, register a guarantee online or email a friend, you could be providing retailers with information that allows them to target

case study

The Weather Channel

US TV network The Weather Channel invites web-users to set up their own customised weather page with maps relating to their city and region. The website requests details such as the user's age, sex, hobbies and income. This site has proved incredibly popular. However, users may not be aware that the site is also a means of gathering information which can then be used to target ads at groups defined by age, gender, income, interests and location. Soon after the service was launched, Todd Walrath, a Weather Channel director, commented: "For the first time, we know who people are."

you personally. Interactive software allows advertisers instant access to customer choices, which helps them to review the effectiveness of advertising. Advertisers say tailoring ads to customers' tastes allows them to avoid wasting people's time with ads that won't be of interest. Critics point out that people are not always aware that information is being gathered, stored and used by advertisers. This can be particularly true of websites aimed at children. Many people feel that some interactive advertising is an invasion of privacy.

The Internet is not the only example of new technology being used to gather personal data. At supermarket checkouts, scanning barcodes and store cards, such as Nectar, allows retailers to determine shoppers' choices so they can tailor ads to the customers' tastes. As with online screening, some people feel that because this may happen without people's knowledge, it is an invasion of privacy.

▼ Online advertising such as spam may result in young people seeing inappropriate material. Young users may also not be aware that information on their surfing and spending behaviour is being gathered via cookies.

Advertising: For and against

Advertising is part of our everyday lives. In future, it will continue to evolve to suit changing needs and make use of new technologies. Just as advertising will remain an essential part of our culture, so the debate about it will continue, with many people holding strong views for or against.

Economic effects

Advertising has far-reaching economic effects. In future it will continue to generate huge sums for companies and also governments through taxes. The industry will continue to provide millions of jobs. Almost all companies use some form of advertising, and without it, the economy as we know it would collapse.

Advertising covers about 75 per cent of the running costs of newspapers and magazines. It funds commercial radio, TV and the Internet. Without advertising most media would not exist. Many people believe that advertising influences the

▼ The American online retailer Amazon has expanded greatly since its launch in 1995, partly thanks to inventive advertising. It originally sold just books but soon diversified, and now sells a huge range of products.

content of the press and other commercial media. They believe that it "lowers the tone" of TV programming, reducing the number of educational and cultural programmes in favour of entertainment. Most media deny that they allow advertisers to influence content. They say that if the only newspapers and news channels were funded by governments, it could lead to censorship.

Manufacturers say that advertising can lead to product improvement. For example, if one company introduces a feature that proves popular when advertised, other manufacturers may well make similar improvements. Critics say that the high cost of advertising allows big firms to dominate the market. However, the relatively low cost of some forms of advertising, including the Internet, allows smaller companies to compete.

Ethical concerns

Most people acknowledge that advertising influences social habits and public opinion. People disagree, however, whether this is a good thing or not. Critics of the industry say advertising can be misleading and manipulative, exploiting vulnerable consumers, such as children. They maintain that it creates envy and encourages overspending, as well as encouraging poor dietary habits and obesity, particularly among young people.

Advertisers say that ads provide entertainment and useful information. Commercial advertising presents shoppers with choice, so they can select the best. Few people would deny that public service ads are educational, while charity ads increase our understanding of other groups and cultures. They also arouse "positive" emotions such as generosity and compassion. The subject of aiming advertising at children is especially controversial. Some people feel it encourages young people to become dissatisfied and materialistic. Advertisers say it helps to prepare young people to take their place as consumers in a consumer society.

summary

▶ Online advertising is the fastest growing sector of advertising.

▶ Modern technology allows advertisers to monitor customers' tastes so they can target advertising at individuals. Many people feel this is an invasion of privacy.

Glossary

Advertising copy The printed text used in an advert.

Advertising to sales ratio The percentage of the unit cost made by advertising.

Brand A trademark, product line or most usually, a particular product marketed by a manufacturer.

Brand image The image an advertiser gives to a product in order to sell it. Brand image has been called the "personality" of a product.

Branding strategy How a product is marketed.

Channel A type of media, such as television, newspapers or the Internet.

Consumer A person who buys goods or services.

Cookie A small file placed on a user's computer that enables the operator to recognise the user.

Corporate Relating to a business.

Corporate image The image a company has with the general public. Some companies try to improve their image through advertising.

Demographics The study of human populations and groups in society.

Direct mail Advertising sent to homes.

Endorsement When a product is backed by a celebrity or figure of authority, such as a doctor.

Logo A symbol or word that represents a company or product.

Market research A survey of what consumers want.

Mass media Any media that reaches a mass audience, such as press and TV.

Obesity Being overweight.

Nostalgia Thinking fondly about the past.

Positioning The aiming of a product at a particular group of consumers.

Product placement When an advertiser pays for a product to appear in a film or TV show.

Regulator An organisation that regulates an industry or practice.

Repositioning When an advertiser decides to target a product at a different group of consumers and changes the brand image.

Shill When a person works with a seller, acting as an enthusiastic customer to entice or encourage others.

Slogan A short phrase which sums up the message of an advertiser.

Soft sell The advertising technique of subtly selling a brand or product.

Spam Unsolicited emails.

Stereotype A standardised and over-simplified representation of a particular group.

Subliminal advertising Advertising messages flashed very briefly on a screen that may help to persuade consumers to buy.

Telesales When advertisers sell or market products or services using the telephone.

Testimonial When a product is backed by a celebrity or authority figure.

USP Short for Unique Selling Proposition – the quality used to distinguish a product from others that are similar.

Unit cost The cost of manufacturing a product per item.

Voiceover An unidentified voice used in a film, TV or radio programme.

Timeline

From c 700 BCE Greeks and Romans advertise shops and services using signs (because few people can read). In Ancient Egypt, criers are used to advertise goods.

From c 900 CE Criers are hired by merchants in medieval Europe to advertise goods and prices at markets.

1440s The invention of printing paves the way for advertising in handbills, newssheets and newspapers.

1472 William Caxton prints the first ad in English.

1622 The first weekly newssheet is published in the UK.

1704 The first newspaper ad appears in an American newspaper.

1800s Growth of poster advertising.

1804 The first US ad agency is formed by Volney Palmer. By 1900 ad agencies are writing most advertising copy for companies.

1906 First ad for Kellogg's Cornflakes appears. By 1915 Kellogg's are spending US$1 million a year on advertising.

1920s Commercial radio stations start up and soon become an important channel for advertising.

1950s Television provides a new medium for advertising.

1957 Vance Packard's book *The Hidden Persuaders* claims that advertisers use psychological techniques to manipulate the public into buying.

1980s New channels for advertising develop, including cinema and supermarket radio in the US.

1993 Invention of the World Wide Web paves the way for online advertising.

1999 Money spent on Internet advertising exceeds US$2 billion.

1996 First ad, for the soft drink Pepsi, appears in space.

2004 The social network service and website Facebook is launched and soon gains popularity. Global companies not only place ads on the site, but also create profiles that customers can follow, receiving regular updates about products.

2006 The social networking site Twitter is launched, and quickly becomes popular worldwide. Companies start using it to advertise and raise awareness of their brands.

2008 Internet advertising including on social network sites helps Barack Obama to mobilise US voters and win the American presidential campaign.

Further information

Books

Laura Hensley, *Advertising Attack*
(Raintree, 2010)

Clive Gifford, *Advertising and Marketing*
(Heinemann Library, 2006)

Rosie Wilson, *Global Industries Uncovered:
The Media and Communications Industry*
(Wayland, 2009)

Websites

Advertising Age, advertising and marketing
news magazine: http://www.adage.com/

Adslogans, an archive of advertising slogans:
http://www.adslogans.co.uk/

Adflip, archive of advertising including by
decade: http://www.adflip.com/index.php

Regulators:

Advertising Standards Agency, UK:
http://www.asa.org.uk/

American Advertising Federation:
http://www.aaf.org/

Advertising Federation of Australia:
http://www.afa.org.au/index.aspx

Index

Ethical Debates

Contents of new titles in the series: